A
BEER
JOURNAL

Commonwealth Editions
an imprint of Applewood Books
Carlisle, Massachusetts

BEER NOTES

All of us remember our first beer. Where we were and when we had it. Maybe who we were with. Time—or the beer—probably has made some of the specifics hazy, but for those of us who like drinking beer, the memory usually brings a smile to our faces. Beer, or the mere thought of it, tends to do that.

Drinkers of a certain age got their first tastes from now defunct brands like Brown Derby or Olympia, Jax or Falstaff, while old-school suds like Schaefer, Dixie, Ballantine, Schmidt, Hamm's, Rheingold, Old Style, Shiner Bock, Narragansett, and Lucky are still being imbibed by new generations in various regions of the country. Add in popular giants like Miller High Life, Pabst Blue Ribbon, Schlitz, Budweiser, Busch and Coors, along with shelves full of light beers, and you've got a pretty good percentage of what beer drinkers are chugging, sipping or throwing back nowadays.

But beers, and beer drinking, have come a long way. Craft beers and breweries have taken the world by storm over the past two decades, offering an unimaginably large number of choices—pale ales, IPAs, dark lagers, tart ales, and on and on. With more than 3,000 craft brewers now on the scene, the options, fun as they are, can be overwhelming. How do you keep up – and keep track? That's where *A Beer Journal* comes in.

This handy, portable, personal journal is the perfect companion for your next visit to the local brew pub—or the cool new brewery you've just discovered. It's also a great way to keep track of that bottle or can of craft beer you picked up at your favorite store or in your travels, which could be brewed in Texas, California, Massachusetts or any state in between.

Sure, you can track your beer likes and dislikes on an app, but since beer drinking isn't a virtual sport, why not capture your thoughts about a new porter or double IPA on something just as real? And that splash of stout that landed on the page as you're rating it? That's called adding character to your journal.

Think of the pages of *A Beer Journal* as a way for you to not only note the specifics of what you've tasted—color, style, taste—but as your personal take on the tap room experience. Great space? Friendly bartenders? Cool crowd? Good food? You can do the same thing with that limited-run pint of IPA you brought home after work. Memorable can design? Terrific with fish? Too tasty to share?

So use the pages of *A Beer Journal* however you want: sketch your glass or coaster, snap a Polaroid and glue it in, jot down contact info for folks you meet at the bar. It's your journal, so do what all of us beer drinkers like to do: have fun!

—Bob Young

IN THE BAG

BEERS AT HOME

_____

NAME OF BEER

_____

BREWER/LOCATION

_____

BOTTLE OR CAN

_____

SIZE

_____

BEER STYLE

_____

ABV

_____

RATING (1 TO 5)

_____

NAME OF BEER

_____

BREWER/LOCATION

_____

BOTTLE OR CAN

_____

SIZE

_____

BEER STYLE

_____

ABV

_____

RATING (1 TO 5)

BEERS AT HOME

_____

NAME OF BEER

_____

BREWER/LOCATION

_____

BOTTLE OR CAN

_____

SIZE

_____

BEER STYLE

_____

ABV

_____

RATING (1 TO 5)

_____

NAME OF BEER

_____

BREWER/LOCATION

_____

BOTTLE OR CAN

_____

SIZE

_____

BEER STYLE

_____

ABV

_____

RATING (1 TO 5)

NAME OF BEER

BREWER/LOCATION

BOTTLE OR CAN

SIZE

BEER STYLE

ABV

RATING (I TO 5)

NAME OF BEER

BREWER/LOCATION

BOTTLE OR CAN

SIZE

BEER STYLE

ABV

RATING (I TO 5)

BEERS AT HOME

NAME OF BEER

BREWER/LOCATION

BOTTLE OR CAN

SIZE

BEER STYLE

ABV

RATING (I TO 5)

NAME OF BEER

BREWER/LOCATION

BOTTLE OR CAN

SIZE

BEER STYLE

ABV

RATING (I TO 5)

"When I die, I want to decompose in a barrel of porter and have it served in all the pubs in Dublin. I wonder would they know it was me?"

—J.P. Donleavy

BEERS AT HOME

NAME OF BEER

BREWER/LOCATION

BOTTLE OR CAN

SIZE

BEER STYLE

ABV

RATING (1 TO 5)

NAME OF BEER

BREWER/LOCATION

BOTTLE OR CAN

SIZE

BEER STYLE

ABV

RATING (1 TO 5)

NAME OF BEER

BREWER/LOCATION

BOTTLE OR CAN

SIZE

BEER STYLE

ABV

RATING (1 TO 5)

NAME OF BEER

BREWER/LOCATION

BOTTLE OR CAN

SIZE

BEER STYLE

ABV

RATING (1 TO 5)

BEERS AT HOME

NAME OF BEER

BREWER/LOCATION

BOTTLE OR CAN

SIZE

BEER STYLE

ABV

RATING (1 TO 5)

NAME OF BEER

BREWER/LOCATION

BOTTLE OR CAN

SIZE

BEER STYLE

ABV

RATING (1 TO 5)

IN THE BAG

NAME OF BEER

BREWER/LOCATION

BOTTLE OR CAN

SIZE

BEER STYLE

ABV

RATING (1 TO 5)

NAME OF BEER

BREWER/LOCATION

BOTTLE OR CAN

SIZE

BEER STYLE

ABV

RATING (1 TO 5)

"Beer's intellectual. What a shame so many idiots drink it."
—Ray Bradbury

_____
NAME OF BEER

_____
BREWER/LOCATION

_____
BOTTLE OR CAN

_____
SIZE

_____
BEER STYLE

_____
ABV

_____
RATING (1 TO 5)

_____
NAME OF BEER

_____
BREWER/LOCATION

_____
BOTTLE OR CAN

_____
SIZE

_____
BEER STYLE

_____
ABV

_____
RATING (1 TO 5)

BEERS AT HOME

NAME OF BEER

BREWER/LOCATION

BOTTLE OR CAN

SIZE

BEER STYLE

ABV

RATING (1 TO 5)

NAME OF BEER

BREWER/LOCATION

BOTTLE OR CAN

SIZE

BEER STYLE

ABV

RATING (1 TO 5)

NAME OF BEER

BREWER/LOCATION

BOTTLE OR CAN

SIZE

BEER STYLE

ABV

RATING (1 TO 5)

NAME OF BEER

BREWER/LOCATION

BOTTLE OR CAN

SIZE

BEER STYLE

ABV

RATING (1 TO 5)

BEERS AT HOME

NAME OF BEER

BREWER/LOCATION

BOTTLE OR CAN

SIZE

BEER STYLE

ABV

RATING (1 TO 5)

NAME OF BEER

BREWER/LOCATION

BOTTLE OR CAN

SIZE

BEER STYLE

ABV

RATING (1 TO 5)

"God has a brown voice, as soft and full as beer."
—Anne Sexton

BEERS AT HOME

NAME OF BEER

BREWER/LOCATION

BOTTLE OR CAN

SIZE

BEER STYLE

ABV

RATING (1 TO 5)

NAME OF BEER

BREWER/LOCATION

BOTTLE OR CAN

SIZE

BEER STYLE

ABV

RATING (1 TO 5)

NAME OF BEER

BREWER/LOCATION

BOTTLE OR CAN

SIZE

BEER STYLE

ABV

RATING (1 TO 5)

NAME OF BEER

BREWER/LOCATION

BOTTLE OR CAN

SIZE

BEER STYLE

ABV

RATING (1 TO 5)

BEERS AT HOME

NAME OF BEER

BREWER/LOCATION

BOTTLE OR CAN

SIZE

BEER STYLE

ABV

RATING (1 TO 5)

NAME OF BEER

BREWER/LOCATION

BOTTLE OR CAN

SIZE

BEER STYLE

ABV

RATING (1 TO 5)

IN THE BAG

_____
NAME OF BEER

_____
BREWER/LOCATION

_____
BOTTLE OR CAN

_____
SIZE

_____
BEER STYLE

_____
ABV

_____
RATING (1 TO 5)

_____
NAME OF BEER

_____
BREWER/LOCATION

_____
BOTTLE OR CAN

_____
SIZE

_____
BEER STYLE

_____
ABV

_____
RATING (1 TO 5)

"I've only been in love with a beer bottle and a mirror."
—Sid Vicious

NAME OF BEER

BREWER/LOCATION

BOTTLE OR CAN

SIZE

BEER STYLE

ABV

RATING (1 TO 5)

NAME OF BEER

BREWER/LOCATION

BOTTLE OR CAN

SIZE

BEER STYLE

ABV

RATING (1 TO 5)

BEERS AT HOME

NAME OF BEER

BREWER/LOCATION

BOTTLE OR CAN

SIZE

BEER STYLE

ABV

RATING (I TO 5)

NAME OF BEER

BREWER/LOCATION

BOTTLE OR CAN

SIZE

BEER STYLE

ABV

RATING (I TO 5)

NAME OF BEER

BREWER/LOCATION

BOTTLE OR CAN

SIZE

BEER STYLE

ABV

RATING (I TO 5)

NAME OF BEER

BREWER/LOCATION

BOTTLE OR CAN

SIZE

BEER STYLE

ABV

RATING (I TO 5)

BEERS AT HOME

NAME OF BEER

BREWER/LOCATION

BOTTLE OR CAN

SIZE

BEER STYLE

ABV

RATING (I TO 5)

NAME OF BEER

BREWER/LOCATION

BOTTLE OR CAN

SIZE

BEER STYLE

ABV

RATING (I TO 5)

"He was a wise man who invented beer."

—Plato

BEERS AT HOME

_____
NAME OF BEER

_____
BREWER/LOCATION

_____
BOTTLE OR CAN

_____
SIZE

_____
BEER STYLE

_____
ABV

_____
RATING (1 TO 5)

_____
NAME OF BEER

_____
BREWER/LOCATION

_____
BOTTLE OR CAN

_____
SIZE

_____
BEER STYLE

_____
ABV

_____
RATING (1 TO 5)

NAME OF BEER

BREWER/LOCATION

BOTTLE OR CAN

SIZE

BEER STYLE

ABV

RATING (I TO 5)

NAME OF BEER

BREWER/LOCATION

BOTTLE OR CAN

SIZE

BEER STYLE

ABV

RATING (I TO 5)

BEERS AT HOME

_____

NAME OF BEER

_____

BREWER/LOCATION

_____

BOTTLE OR CAN

_____

SIZE

_____

BEER STYLE

_____

ABV

_____

RATING (1 TO 5)

_____

NAME OF BEER

_____

BREWER/LOCATION

_____

BOTTLE OR CAN

_____

SIZE

_____

BEER STYLE

_____

ABV

_____

RATING (1 TO 5)

NAME OF BEER

BREWER/LOCATION

BOTTLE OR CAN

SIZE

BEER STYLE

ABV

RATING (1 TO 5)

NAME OF BEER

BREWER/LOCATION

BOTTLE OR CAN

SIZE

BEER STYLE

ABV

RATING (1 TO 5)

"Beer, it's the best damn drink in the world."
—Jack Nicholson

NAME OF BEER

BREWER/LOCATION

BOTTLE OR CAN

SIZE

BEER STYLE

ABV

RATING (1 TO 5)

NAME OF BEER

BREWER/LOCATION

BOTTLE OR CAN

SIZE

BEER STYLE

ABV

RATING (1 TO 5)

NAME OF BEER

BREWER/LOCATION

BOTTLE OR CAN

SIZE

BEER STYLE

ABV

RATING (I TO 5)

NAME OF BEER

BREWER/LOCATION

BOTTLE OR CAN

SIZE

BEER STYLE

ABV

RATING (I TO 5)

NAME OF BEER

BREWER/LOCATION

BOTTLE OR CAN

SIZE

BEER STYLE

ABV

RATING (1 TO 5)

NAME OF BEER

BREWER/LOCATION

BOTTLE OR CAN

SIZE

BEER STYLE

ABV

RATING (1 TO 5)

BEERS AT HOME

NAME OF BEER

BREWER/LOCATION

BOTTLE OR CAN

SIZE

BEER STYLE

ABV

RATING (I TO 5)

NAME OF BEER

BREWER/LOCATION

BOTTLE OR CAN

SIZE

BEER STYLE

ABV

RATING (I TO 5)

"There is nothing in the world like the first taste of beer."
—John Steinbeck

BEERS AT HOME

NAME OF BEER

BREWER/LOCATION

BOTTLE OR CAN

SIZE

BEER STYLE

ABV

RATING (1 TO 5)

NAME OF BEER

BREWER/LOCATION

BOTTLE OR CAN

SIZE

BEER STYLE

ABV

RATING (1 TO 5)

NAME OF BEER

BREWER/LOCATION

BOTTLE OR CAN

SIZE

BEER STYLE

ABV

RATING (1 TO 5)

NAME OF BEER

BREWER/LOCATION

BOTTLE OR CAN

SIZE

BEER STYLE

ABV

RATING (1 TO 5)

BEERS AT HOME

NAME OF BEER

BREWER/LOCATION

BOTTLE OR CAN

SIZE

BEER STYLE

ABV

RATING (1 TO 5)

NAME OF BEER

BREWER/LOCATION

BOTTLE OR CAN

SIZE

BEER STYLE

ABV

RATING (1 TO 5)

NAME OF BEER

BREWER/LOCATION

BOTTLE OR CAN

SIZE

BEER STYLE

ABV

RATING (I TO 5)

NAME OF BEER

BREWER/LOCATION

BOTTLE OR CAN

SIZE

BEER STYLE

ABV

RATING (I TO 5)

"What care I how time advances? I am drinking ale today."
—Edgar Allan Poe

IN THE BAG

NAME OF BEER

BREWER/LOCATION

BOTTLE OR CAN

SIZE

BEER STYLE

ABV

RATING (1 TO 5)

NAME OF BEER

BREWER/LOCATION

BOTTLE OR CAN

SIZE

BEER STYLE

ABV

RATING (1 TO 5)

BEERS AT HOME

NAME OF BEER

BREWER/LOCATION

BOTTLE OR CAN

SIZE

BEER STYLE

ABV

RATING (1 TO 5)

NAME OF BEER

BREWER/LOCATION

BOTTLE OR CAN

SIZE

BEER STYLE

ABV

RATING (1 TO 5)

NAME OF BEER

BREWER/LOCATION

BOTTLE OR CAN

SIZE

BEER STYLE

ABV

RATING (1 TO 5)

NAME OF BEER

BREWER/LOCATION

BOTTLE OR CAN

SIZE

BEER STYLE

ABV

RATING (1 TO 5)

BEERS AT HOME

NAME OF BEER

BREWER/LOCATION

BOTTLE OR CAN

SIZE

BEER STYLE

ABV

RATING (1 TO 5)

NAME OF BEER

BREWER/LOCATION

BOTTLE OR CAN

SIZE

BEER STYLE

ABV

RATING (1 TO 5)

"A man who lies about beer makes enemies."
—Stephen King

BEERS AT HOME

NAME OF BEER

BREWER/LOCATION

BOTTLE OR CAN

SIZE

BEER STYLE

ABV

RATING (1 TO 5)

NAME OF BEER

BREWER/LOCATION

BOTTLE OR CAN

SIZE

BEER STYLE

ABV

RATING (1 TO 5)

NAME OF BEER

BREWER/LOCATION

BOTTLE OR CAN

SIZE

BEER STYLE

ABV

RATING (1 TO 5)

NAME OF BEER

BREWER/LOCATION

BOTTLE OR CAN

SIZE

BEER STYLE

ABV

RATING (1 TO 5)

BEERS AT HOME

NAME OF BEER

BREWER/LOCATION

BOTTLE OR CAN

SIZE

BEER STYLE

ABV

RATING (1 TO 5)

NAME OF BEER

BREWER/LOCATION

BOTTLE OR CAN

SIZE

BEER STYLE

ABV

RATING (1 TO 5)

NAME OF BEER

BREWER/LOCATION

BOTTLE OR CAN

SIZE

BEER STYLE

ABV

RATING (1 TO 5)

NAME OF BEER

BREWER/LOCATION

BOTTLE OR CAN

SIZE

BEER STYLE

ABV

RATING (1 TO 5)

"For a quart of Ale is a dish for a king."
—William Shakespeare

NAME OF BEER

BREWER/LOCATION

BOTTLE OR CAN

SIZE

BEER STYLE

ABV

RATING (1 TO 5)

NAME OF BEER

BREWER/LOCATION

BOTTLE OR CAN

SIZE

BEER STYLE

ABV

RATING (1 TO 5)

FROM TAP TO TAP

BEERS AT THE BREWERY

NAME OF BEER

BREWER/LOCATION

BOTTLE OR CAN

SIZE

BEER STYLE

ABV

RATING (I TO 5)

NAME OF BEER

BREWER/LOCATION

BOTTLE OR CAN

SIZE

BEER STYLE

ABV

RATING (I TO 5)

BEERS AT THE BREWERY

NAME OF BEER

BREWER/LOCATION

BOTTLE OR CAN

SIZE

BEER STYLE

ABV

RATING (I TO 5)

NAME OF BEER

BREWER/LOCATION

BOTTLE OR CAN

SIZE

BEER STYLE

ABV

RATING (I TO 5)

NAME OF BEER

BREWER/LOCATION

BOTTLE OR CAN

SIZE

BEER STYLE

ABV

RATING (1 TO 5)

NAME OF BEER

BREWER/LOCATION

BOTTLE OR CAN

SIZE

BEER STYLE

ABV

RATING (1 TO 5)

NAME OF BEER

BREWER/LOCATION

BOTTLE OR CAN

SIZE

BEER STYLE

ABV

RATING (1 TO 5)

NAME OF BEER

BREWER/LOCATION

BOTTLE OR CAN

SIZE

BEER STYLE

ABV

RATING (1 TO 5)

*"Without question, the greatest invention
in the history of mankind is beer.
Oh, I grant you that the wheel was also a fine invention, but the
wheel does not go nearly as well with pizza."*
—Dave Barry

BEERS AT THE BREWERY

NAME OF BEER

BREWER/LOCATION

BOTTLE OR CAN

SIZE

BEER STYLE

ABV

RATING (1 TO 5)

NAME OF BEER

BREWER/LOCATION

BOTTLE OR CAN

SIZE

BEER STYLE

ABV

RATING (1 TO 5)

NAME OF BEER

BREWER/LOCATION

BOTTLE OR CAN

SIZE

BEER STYLE

ABV

RATING (1 TO 5)

NAME OF BEER

BREWER/LOCATION

BOTTLE OR CAN

SIZE

BEER STYLE

ABV

RATING (1 TO 5)

BEERS AT THE BREWERY

NAME OF BEER

BREWER/LOCATION

BOTTLE OR CAN

SIZE

BEER STYLE

ABV

RATING (1 TO 5)

NAME OF BEER

BREWER/LOCATION

BOTTLE OR CAN

SIZE

BEER STYLE

ABV

RATING (1 TO 5)

NAME OF BEER

BREWER/LOCATION

BOTTLE OR CAN

SIZE

BEER STYLE

ABV

RATING (1 TO 5)

NAME OF BEER

BREWER/LOCATION

BOTTLE OR CAN

SIZE

BEER STYLE

ABV

RATING (1 TO 5)

"I work until beer o'clock."
—Stephen King

NAME OF BEER

BREWER/LOCATION

BOTTLE OR CAN

SIZE

BEER STYLE

ABV

RATING (1 TO 5)

NAME OF BEER

BREWER/LOCATION

BOTTLE OR CAN

SIZE

BEER STYLE

ABV

RATING (1 TO 5)

BEERS AT THE BREWERY

NAME OF BEER

BREWER/LOCATION

BOTTLE OR CAN

SIZE

BEER STYLE

ABV

RATING (1 TO 5)

NAME OF BEER

BREWER/LOCATION

BOTTLE OR CAN

SIZE

BEER STYLE

ABV

RATING (1 TO 5)

NAME OF BEER

BREWER/LOCATION

BOTTLE OR CAN

SIZE

BEER STYLE

ABV

RATING (1 TO 5)

NAME OF BEER

BREWER/LOCATION

BOTTLE OR CAN

SIZE

BEER STYLE

ABV

RATING (1 TO 5)

BEERS AT THE BREWERY

NAME OF BEER

BREWER/LOCATION

BOTTLE OR CAN

SIZE

BEER STYLE

ABV

RATING (1 TO 5)

NAME OF BEER

BREWER/LOCATION

BOTTLE OR CAN

SIZE

BEER STYLE

ABV

RATING (1 TO 5)

"Milk is for babies. When you grow up you have to drink beer."
—Arnold Schwarzenegger

NAME OF BEER

BREWER/LOCATION

BOTTLE OR CAN

SIZE

BEER STYLE

ABV

RATING (1 TO 5)

NAME OF BEER

BREWER/LOCATION

BOTTLE OR CAN

SIZE

BEER STYLE

ABV

RATING (1 TO 5)

NAME OF BEER

BREWER/LOCATION

BOTTLE OR CAN

SIZE

BEER STYLE

ABV

RATING (I TO 5)

NAME OF BEER

BREWER/LOCATION

BOTTLE OR CAN

SIZE

BEER STYLE

ABV

RATING (I TO 5)

BEERS AT THE BREWERY

NAME OF BEER

BREWER/LOCATION

BOTTLE OR CAN

SIZE

BEER STYLE

ABV

RATING (I TO 5)

NAME OF BEER

BREWER/LOCATION

BOTTLE OR CAN

SIZE

BEER STYLE

ABV

RATING (I TO 5)

NAME OF BEER

BREWER/LOCATION

BOTTLE OR CAN

SIZE

BEER STYLE

ABV

RATING (1 TO 5)

NAME OF BEER

BREWER/LOCATION

BOTTLE OR CAN

SIZE

BEER STYLE

ABV

RATING (1 TO 5)

"There is an ancient Celtic axiom that says
'Good people drink good beer.' Which is true, then as now.
Just look around you in any public barroom and you will quickly see:
Bad people drink bad beer. Think about it."
—Hunter S. Thompson

NAME OF BEER

BREWER/LOCATION

BOTTLE OR CAN

SIZE

BEER STYLE

ABV

RATING (1 TO 5)

NAME OF BEER

BREWER/LOCATION

BOTTLE OR CAN

SIZE

BEER STYLE

ABV

RATING (1 TO 5)

NAME OF BEER

BREWER/LOCATION

BOTTLE OR CAN

SIZE

BEER STYLE

ABV

RATING (1 TO 5)

NAME OF BEER

BREWER/LOCATION

BOTTLE OR CAN

SIZE

BEER STYLE

ABV

RATING (1 TO 5)

NAME OF BEER

BREWER/LOCATION

BOTTLE OR CAN

SIZE

BEER STYLE

ABV

RATING (1 TO 5)

NAME OF BEER

BREWER/LOCATION

BOTTLE OR CAN

SIZE

BEER STYLE

ABV

RATING (1 TO 5)

BEERS AT THE BREWERY

NAME OF BEER

BREWER/LOCATION

BOTTLE OR CAN

SIZE

BEER STYLE

ABV

RATING (1 TO 5)

NAME OF BEER

BREWER/LOCATION

BOTTLE OR CAN

SIZE

BEER STYLE

ABV

RATING (1 TO 5)

"You can't be a real country unless you have a beer and an airline. It helps if you have some kind of a football team, or some nuclear weapons, but at the very least you need a beer."

—Frank Zappa

BEERS AT THE BREWERY

NAME OF BEER

BREWER/LOCATION

BOTTLE OR CAN

SIZE

BEER STYLE

ABV

RATING (1 TO 5)

NAME OF BEER

BREWER/LOCATION

BOTTLE OR CAN

SIZE

BEER STYLE

ABV

RATING (1 TO 5)

_____

NAME OF BEER

_____

BREWER/LOCATION

_____

BOTTLE OR CAN

_____

SIZE

_____

BEER STYLE

_____

ABV

_____

RATING (1 TO 5)

_____

NAME OF BEER

_____

BREWER/LOCATION

_____

BOTTLE OR CAN

_____

SIZE

_____

BEER STYLE

_____

ABV

_____

RATING (1 TO 5)

NAME OF BEER

BREWER/LOCATION

BOTTLE OR CAN

SIZE

BEER STYLE

ABV

RATING (1 TO 5)

NAME OF BEER

BREWER/LOCATION

BOTTLE OR CAN

SIZE

BEER STYLE

ABV

RATING (1 TO 5)

NAME OF BEER

BREWER/LOCATION

BOTTLE OR CAN

SIZE

BEER STYLE

ABV

RATING (I TO 5)

NAME OF BEER

BREWER/LOCATION

BOTTLE OR CAN

SIZE

BEER STYLE

ABV

RATING (I TO 5)

"Beer: So much more than a breakfast drink."
—Homer Simpson

_____

NAME OF BEER

_____

BREWER/LOCATION

_____

BOTTLE OR CAN

_____

SIZE

_____

BEER STYLE

_____

ABV

_____

RATING (1 TO 5)

_____

NAME OF BEER

_____

BREWER/LOCATION

_____

BOTTLE OR CAN

_____

SIZE

_____

BEER STYLE

_____

ABV

_____

RATING (1 TO 5)

BEERS AT THE BREWERY

NAME OF BEER

BREWER/LOCATION

BOTTLE OR CAN

SIZE

BEER STYLE

ABV

RATING (1 TO 5)

NAME OF BEER

BREWER/LOCATION

BOTTLE OR CAN

SIZE

BEER STYLE

ABV

RATING (1 TO 5)

_____
NAME OF BEER

_____
BREWER/LOCATION

_____
BOTTLE OR CAN

_____
SIZE

_____
BEER STYLE

_____
ABV

_____
RATING (1 TO 5)

_____
NAME OF BEER

_____
BREWER/LOCATION

_____
BOTTLE OR CAN

_____
SIZE

_____
BEER STYLE

_____
ABV

_____
RATING (1 TO 5)

BEERS AT THE BREWERY

NAME OF BEER

BREWER/LOCATION

BOTTLE OR CAN

SIZE

BEER STYLE

ABV

RATING (I TO 5)

NAME OF BEER

BREWER/LOCATION

BOTTLE OR CAN

SIZE

BEER STYLE

ABV

RATING (I TO 5)

*"Nothing ever tasted better than a cold beer
on a beautiful afternoon with nothing to look forward to
than more of the same."*
—Hugo Hood

NAME OF BEER

BREWER/LOCATION

BOTTLE OR CAN

SIZE

BEER STYLE

ABV

RATING (1 TO 5)

NAME OF BEER

BREWER/LOCATION

BOTTLE OR CAN

SIZE

BEER STYLE

ABV

RATING (1 TO 5)

NAME OF BEER

BREWER/LOCATION

BOTTLE OR CAN

SIZE

BEER STYLE

ABV

RATING (1 TO 5)

NAME OF BEER

BREWER/LOCATION

BOTTLE OR CAN

SIZE

BEER STYLE

ABV

RATING (1 TO 5)

BEERS AT THE BREWERY

NAME OF BEER

BREWER/LOCATION

BOTTLE OR CAN

SIZE

BEER STYLE

ABV

RATING (1 TO 5)

NAME OF BEER

BREWER/LOCATION

BOTTLE OR CAN

SIZE

BEER STYLE

ABV

RATING (1 TO 5)

NAME OF BEER

BREWER/LOCATION

BOTTLE OR CAN

SIZE

BEER STYLE

ABV

RATING (I TO 5)

NAME OF BEER

BREWER/LOCATION

BOTTLE OR CAN

SIZE

BEER STYLE

ABV

RATING (I TO 5)

"I am a firm believer in the people.
If given the truth, they can be depended upon to
meet any national crisis.
The great point is to bring them the real facts, and beer."
—Abraham Lincoln

NAME OF BEER

BREWER/LOCATION

BOTTLE OR CAN

SIZE

BEER STYLE

ABV

RATING (1 TO 5)

NAME OF BEER

BREWER/LOCATION

BOTTLE OR CAN

SIZE

BEER STYLE

ABV

RATING (1 TO 5)

NAME OF BEER

BREWER/LOCATION

BOTTLE OR CAN

SIZE

BEER STYLE

ABV

RATING (1 TO 5)

NAME OF BEER

BREWER/LOCATION

BOTTLE OR CAN

SIZE

BEER STYLE

ABV

RATING (1 TO 5)

NAME OF BEER

BREWER/LOCATION

BOTTLE OR CAN

SIZE

BEER STYLE

ABV

RATING (1 TO 5)

NAME OF BEER

BREWER/LOCATION

BOTTLE OR CAN

SIZE

BEER STYLE

ABV

RATING (1 TO 5)

BEERS AT THE BREWERY

NAME OF BEER

BREWER/LOCATION

BOTTLE OR CAN

SIZE

BEER STYLE

ABV

RATING (1 TO 5)

NAME OF BEER

BREWER/LOCATION

BOTTLE OR CAN

SIZE

BEER STYLE

ABV

RATING (1 TO 5)

"I think it's time for beer."
—Franklin Roosevelt

BEERS AT THE BREWERY

_____

NAME OF BEER

_____

BREWER/LOCATION

_____

BOTTLE OR CAN

_____

SIZE

_____

BEER STYLE

_____

ABV

_____

RATING (1 TO 5)

_____

NAME OF BEER

_____

BREWER/LOCATION

_____

BOTTLE OR CAN

_____

SIZE

_____

BEER STYLE

_____

ABV

_____

RATING (1 TO 5)

NAME OF BEER

BREWER/LOCATION

BOTTLE OR CAN

SIZE

BEER STYLE

ABV

RATING (1 TO 5)

NAME OF BEER

BREWER/LOCATION

BOTTLE OR CAN

SIZE

BEER STYLE

ABV

RATING (1 TO 5)

NAME OF BEER

BREWER/LOCATION

BOTTLE OR CAN

SIZE

BEER STYLE

ABV

RATING (1 TO 5)

NAME OF BEER

BREWER/LOCATION

BOTTLE OR CAN

SIZE

BEER STYLE

ABV

RATING (1 TO 5)

NAME OF BEER

BREWER/LOCATION

BOTTLE OR CAN

SIZE

BEER STYLE

ABV

RATING (I TO 5)

NAME OF BEER

BREWER/LOCATION

BOTTLE OR CAN

SIZE

BEER STYLE

ABV

RATING (I TO 5)

BEER GLOSSARY

ABV (Alcohol by Volume): Measurement of the alcohol content in beer expressed as a percentage of the total volume of the beer.

Ale: A beer type brewed using a process where the yeast gathers and ferments rapidly at the top (top fermentation) at a high temperature. Differs from a lager beer because it's typically more bitter and complex, can have a higher alcohol content, and is served at warmer temperatures.

Bomber: A 22-ounce bottle of beer.

Dry-hopped: A beer to which hops were added after the boiling process in order to increase hop character, including flavors and aromas.

Flight of beer: A group of beers for tasting, usually of various kinds and in smaller amounts.

Gravity: In the context of fermenting alcoholic beverages it refers to specific gravity, or relative density compared to water. A "high gravity" beer is one with a high alcohol content.

Growler: A jug-like container, usually 64 ounces, for carrying draft beer bought at a brewery or pub.

Hops: The herb added to the boiling or fermenting process to impart various levels of bitter aromas and flavors.

IBU (International Bitterness Unit): A system of measuring the hop bitterness in beer.

Imperial: A term used by some brewers to indicate a beer with a higher alcohol level than is usual for a particular style of beer. "Double" is another term indicating the same.

Lager: A beer type produced using a process where the yeast sinks to the bottom (bottom fermentation) and ferments at colder temperatures than ale yeast. Lagers are milder and most often associated with crisp, clean flavors and usually served at colder temperatures than ales.

Malt: Malted cereal grains, primarily barley malt, provide the sugars that are fermented by the yeast in beer. A primary source of beer color and flavor.

Session beers: Typically lower-alcohol beers of various styles, usually under 5% ABV.

Yeast: A fungus that produces, among other things, alcohol and carbonation as it consumes sugar—or ferments. Yeast controls the final stage of the brewing process and determines much of the flavor.

BEER STYLES

These days there is an almost endless variety of beer styles, with most—but not all—of them falling into the lager and ale categories. As craft brewers become more and more imaginative and inventive, the kinds of beers available to sample continue to explode in number, with variation upon variation pushing the envelope of taste, color and alcohol content. Below are descriptions of some of the more familiar styles out there, a good place to start in your personal beer journey. Have a good time tasting the differences!

LAGERS

Bock: Stronger and darker than most lagers, and more malt and less hops. Its even darker cousin, doppelbock ("double bock") has a higher alcohol content.

Golden lagers: Think Budweiser, Miller, Pabst, Michelob and Coors and you've got the most popular beers in America, milder, easy-to-drink brews with a lower alcohol count and refreshing taste, especially on a hot summer day.

Light lagers: Lighter-bodied and lower in calories, "lite" beers brewed mostly by the industry giants are a huge market category that shows no signs of fading.

Oktoberfest lagers: Darker in color with a slightly higher alcohol content and richer flavor, these German-inspired brews hit the taps and shelves every fall.

Pilsners: A hugely popular style around the globe that originated in the Czech Republic in the 17th century, these light, pale-colored beers have more hops than golden lagers but are similarly easy to drink.

ALES

Blonde ale: Sometimes almost lager-like in their lightness, blonde ales have only a touch of hoppy bitterness and can even include a slight taste of fruit in their flavor.

Brown ale: A sweeter, lightly hopped ale with a dark amber or brown color. It originated in England, where it was brewed with 100% brown malt.

IPA (India Pale Ale): Arguably the most popular style of craft beer, IPAs have a more bitter and intense hop flavor than pale ales and often a slightly higher alcohol content.

Kolsch: This crisp German-style ale is similar in lightness to a pilsner lager, but drier and slightly more bitter and tart.

Pale ale: Usually less hoppy than an IPA, pale ales are brewed with roasted malts and have a gold or copper color.

Porter: English brewers added hops to brown ale to create a brew that's sweeter and darker in color than most ales, but with an occasional hop bitterness.

Red ale: More malt flavors than hoppier ales make red ales a smoother alternative to pale ales and IPAs.

Sour ale: This growing category of ales encompasses a range of styles, from gose and lambic to saison and wild ale. What they have in common is experimentation with ingredients that results in tartness, freshness and highly unusual aftertastes.

Stout: Often creamier and heavier than a porter, with little hop flavor, stouts can have higher alcohol levels than other ales.

Wheat beer: This German-derived ale is lighter than a pale ale but is usually unfiltered, giving it a cloudy appearance in the glass or bottle.

Wit: An unfiltered Belgian-style ale with a high level of wheat and usually spiced with one or more herbs.

www.ingramcontent.com/pod-product-compliance
Lightning Source LLC
Chambersburg PA
CBHW040206060426
42445CB00036B/1952